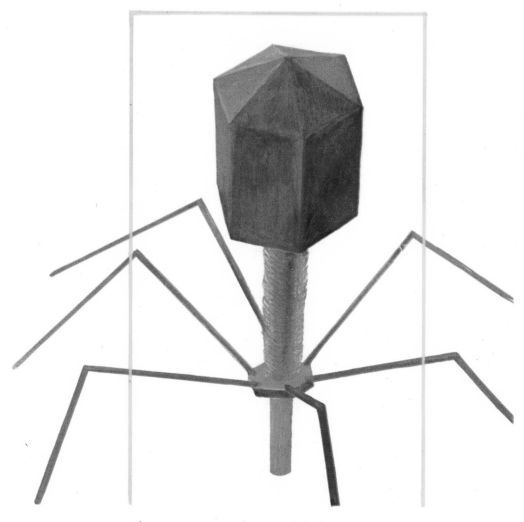

The microscope has enabled man
to understand many of the basic structures
and processes of living things.

"The lens of the microscope may someday reveal the ultimate mystery of life itself."

UNDER THE MICROSCOPE

Photographs and text by
TAY SLOAN
Santa Rosa Junior College
Santa Rosa, California
With DORIS SLOAN

Front matter illustrations by Robert Borja

Drawings by Ned Pankin

CHILDRENS PRESS, Chicago

ACKNOWLEDGMENTS
We thank Dr. Donald M. Hatfield, Director of Audio Visual Education and Supervisor of Secondary Teaching, University of California, for his generous assistance in the preparation of the manuscript.

PICTURE ACKNOWLEDGMENTS
For the microscope slides from which the pictures in *Under the Microscope* were photographed, we wish to thank Dr. William Balamuth, Professor of Zoology, University of California; Ernest Rothart, Instructor in Botany, Santa Rosa Junior College; and Ellis Nixon, Instructor in Zoology, Santa Rosa Junior College. For the black-and-white photographs we wish to thank The American Museum of Natural History; Bausch & Lomb Optical Company; Philips Electronics Instruments, A Division of Philips Electronics and Pharmaceutical Industries Corporation; and Orville Goldner. The microphotographs were taken with the aid of optical systems and illumination by Bausch & Lomb Optical Company. Front matter illustrations by Robert Borja.

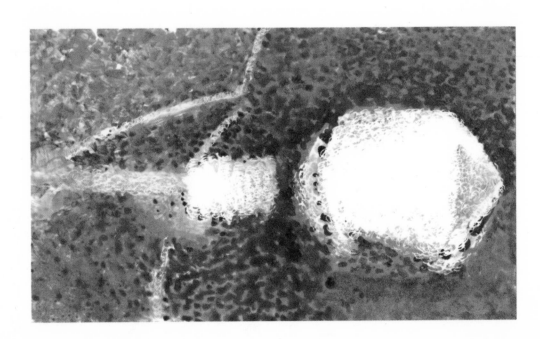

CONTENTS

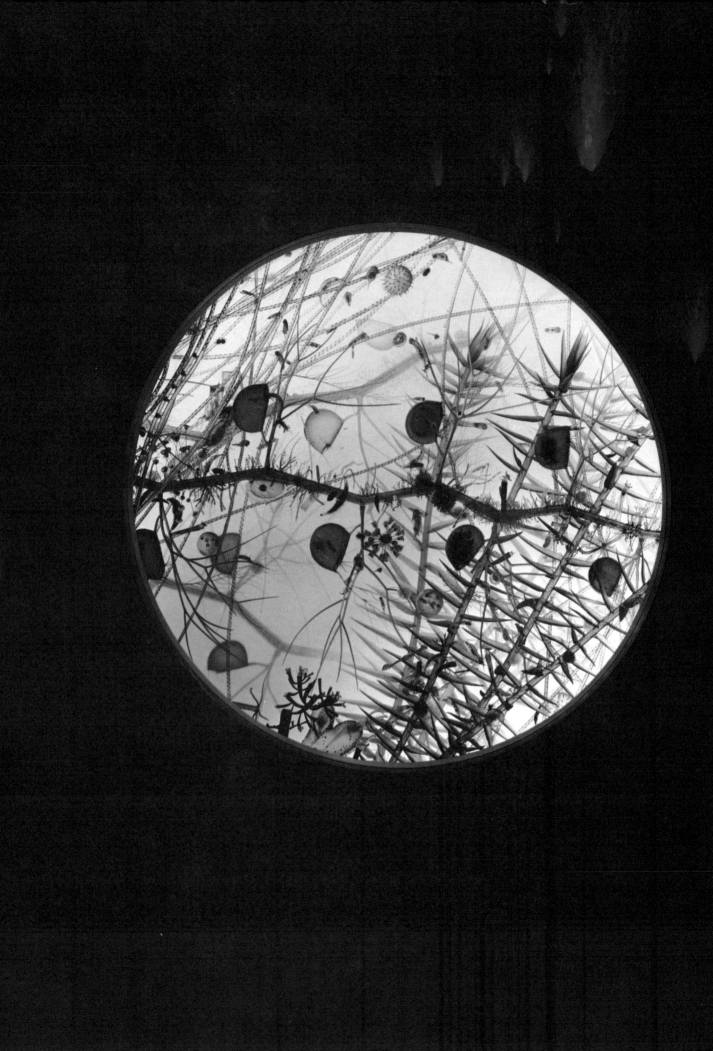

UNDER THE MICROSCOPE

THE EYE IS A WONDERFUL SENSITIVE ORGAN WHICH WE use to explore the world around us. With our eyes we see the endless beauty of colors and forms. We are aware of the depth of space; we understand movement, and, looking at the stars, we sense the vastness of the universe.

Yet, as marvelous as the eye is, it sees only a small part of our world. Human curiosity, however, reaches into the unknown. Where natural human equipment fails, man has invented instruments to help him discover nature's secrets. Two great inventions made in the seventeenth century—the telescope and the microscope—succeeded in extending human vision and knowledge beyond even the most ambitious dreams. First came the telescope, which brought objects in distant space into focus. Observers no longer saw merely the face of the "man" in the moon, but the rugged mountains and giant craters of the eerie lunar surface. And beyond the old imagined limits of the sky, the telescope revealed countless stars. Faint blurs of celestial light became starry galaxies, some larger than our own, some at unbelievable distances. A veil had suddenly lifted on a vast universe previously hidden in the dark reaches of space.

At about the same time, another world unfolded for the scientists who gazed through the newly invented microscope. The tiniest insects, barely visible to the naked eye, suddenly were discovered to have the complex body structures of larger animals. Under the microscope a mere drop of seawater swarmed with countless numbers of astounding creatures. The scientific world expanded almost simultaneously in two different directions.

The tiny world at the bottom of a pond is revealed by the microscope. The saclike objects along the horizontal stem of the bladderwort, a meat-eating water plant, are used to trap rotifers and other microscopic animals living in the pond. The flowerlike structure at the center of the picture is a colony of rotifers with stems joined. The dark areas in the bladderwort's sacs are trapped rotifers.

DEVELOPMENT OF THE MICROSCOPE

The first hint of the possibility of extending man's sight
had come in the thirteenth century when an outstanding scientist
of the Middle Ages, Robert Grosseteste (*GROSS-test*), suggested
using curved glass to magnify small objects and bring distant
ones closer by enlarging their images. It had been known for some
time that lenses could focus the sun's rays and kindle a flame,
but Roger Bacon, another important thirteenth-century scientist and
a follower of Grosseteste, was the first to suggest that outward
curving lenses (convex lenses) could correct faulty eyesight.
By the end of the century, spectacles and magnifying glasses were
being used, especially by the monks who copied manuscripts
by hand in the days before the printing press. By itself, a
magnifying glass can enlarge objects only about ten times their
natural size. Beyond that power, a single lens distorts the image.
So weak an instrument might be adequate for the scholars of
the Middle Ages, but the men who followed would not be satisfied
with its limited capacity.

By the early seventeenth century, Europe was enjoying a
tremendous, dazzling scientific revolution. It was an age of
exploration into unknown corners of physical and natural science.
Scientists were raising important new questions that demanded
answers. They wanted to see more and more detail, to explore
deeper and deeper into the invisible worlds around them. A better
lens than the magnifying glass was needed. Men began to develop a
more delicate, more flexible instrument to bring very small
objects into clear focus.

The earliest microscopes consisted of one or two bits of curved
glass to make an object appear bigger, and a rough adjustment
screw which moved the object up and down to bring it into
focus. With just such a primitive instrument a man named Anton
van Leeuwenhoek (*LAY-ven-hook*) discovered the tiny world
beyond human sight some three hundred years ago. Leeuwenhoek, a
Dutchman who operated a dry-goods business, was endowed
with a probing spirit. His passion was lens grinding, and he
spent all the time he could spare in carefully grinding and polishing
his little lenses by hand. Grinding a lens by hand is a delicate

and lengthy operation, for the surface must be evenly curved and perfectly polished or the object to be viewed will be distorted or blurred.

Leeuwenhoek turned his lenses onto everything imaginable. He looked at a bee stinger, moldy bread, strands of hair, blood from his own finger. Year after year he peered into the world of little things. He ground hundreds of lenses—better than anyone had made before—and built some of them into microscopes. One day he looked at a drop of water from a rain barrel—the purest, clearest water known in those days. To his great astonishment he saw things swimming around in the water. He called these incredibly small, twisting, turning animals "wee beasties."

Leeuwenhoek was the first man to see living creatures too small to be visible to the naked eye, and his report to the world of science caused a great stir. Today we call these tiny animals microbes, and Leeuwenhoek is sometimes known as "the father of microbiology."

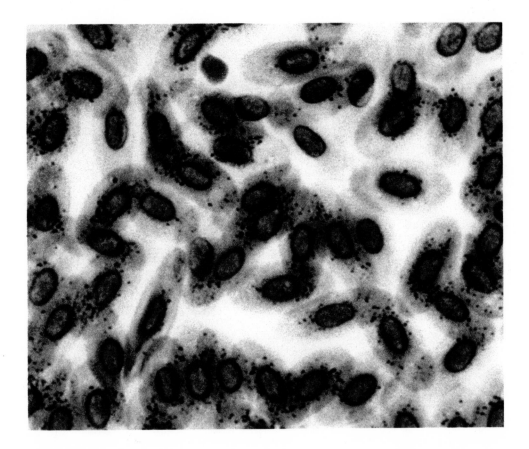

This is a microscopic view of the blood cells of a frog. One of the thousands of amazing subjects Anton van Leeuwenhoek studied under his microscope.

This early compound microscope was used by the English scientist, Robert Hooke. The oil lamp (below) was its light source. A transparent globe of water increased the power of the light given off by the oil lamp. A lens trained this light on the object to be viewed bringing it into sharper focus. The simple microscope (right) was made of a single convex lens and eyepiece.

The microscope opened new avenues of study to the men of the seventeenth and eighteenth centuries. Marcello Malpighi *(mar-CHEL-loh mahl-PEE-ghee)*, a great Italian physiologist, used the microscope to explore the puzzle of the chicken developing inside an egg; he cut away a section of shell and watched through the membrane, which he left untouched. Malpighi studied the cell structure of plants and, in a frog's lung, he saw for the first time in history how blood flows through the capillaries. In England, Nehemiah Grew investigated plant life under the microscope. Jan Swammerdam of Holland studied the life histories of insects. Robert Hooke, another Englishman and a significant figure in many fields of science, examined the compound eye of a fly, the cellular structure of cork, the stinging cells of the nettle plant.

To meet the demand increasingly powerful microscopes were developed, and through the years great progress was made in constucting better, more complex instruments. Today, research microscopes can enlarge an object up to eleven hundred times, and the recently invented electron microscope can multiply objects more than five hundred thousand times. The reason this microscope is so powerful is that electrons have a shorter wave length than light. This means that an electron beam can focus on structures so small or so close together that they would be only a blur when seen through any ordinary research microscope. Through the electron microscope, scientists have discovered what seems to be the final limits of living matter.

The microscope is now an essential tool in chemistry, biology, industrial research, criminal investigation, forestry and agriculture, metallurgy and medicine. Special techniques have been developed for viewing such objects as gems and crystals, polished or etched surfaces, small mechanical parts, whole insects, germinating seeds, feathers and fibers, sections of plant or animal tissues, and living cells.

The usefulness of the microscope increased with the years. Here a doctor of the nineteenth century studies a specimen to search out disease-causing bacteria.

HOW LIVING THINGS REPRODUCE

To see life develop and grow is the greatest miracle brought within reach of man's eyesight by the microscope. Before the microscope's invention, men believed that living things came somehow from non-living matter—rock, water, or fire. The microscope showed that much of life begins in a single-celled egg, often too small to be seen by the eye alone. But even after the microscope had revealed the existence of tiny egg cells, two hundred years passed before scientists began to understand how complex animals could develop from them. For a long time it was believed that the unborn individual was already fully formed inside the egg and that it grew only in size. Less than a hundred years ago, scientists saw the truth with their own eyes. In 1875, a microscope showed for the first time the actual union of egg and sperm (in the sea urchin) and the rapid division and growth which follows immediately. The realization dawned that the egg has a potential for eventually developing from a single cell into one of the complicated creatures of the earth.

Living things have many ways of reproducing their kind. The simplest animals—the single-celled protozoa (proh-toh-ZOH-uh), or "first animals"—reproduce by fission: one individual simply divides to become two. The amoeba (uh-MEE-buh) and the paramecium (pair-uh-MEE-shee-um) are well-known forms of protozoa which reproduce by fission. Bacteria and algae also multiply in this way. In fact, fission is the main method of reproduction found in all single-celled animals and plants.

Another method of reproduction is budding. In this process a new individual grows, like a limb, from the body of its parent. When the bud is mature, it drops off and begins its adult life. Yeast, sponges, sea anemones, and corals reproduce by budding. The freshwater plant spirogyra (spy-roh-JIGH-ruh), a kind of pond scum, can multiply by either method—budding or fission.

Some plants and animals reproduce by regeneration, the growth of a complete organism from one of its parts. When you take a cutting of a garden plant, such as the geranium, it reproduces by regeneration. A starfish or sea star, cut in half, will regenerate to form two new animals. Earthworms can regenerate, and the little flatworm has truly remarkable powers of regeneration, as we shall see.

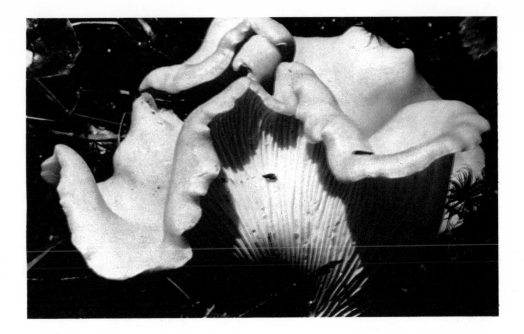

A number of plants—ferns, mushrooms, mosses, molds—
reproduce by means of spores. Other plant cells may grow and
divide to add to some special part of the plant—root, stem, or leaf.
But a spore cell is able to develop into a whole new plant—roots,
stem, leaves, and all! In the mushroom's gills, as many as twenty
thousand spores may grow in a single second on a warm summer
day! Such numbers are necessary for the survival of spore-bearing
plants, since only one in perhaps twenty billion spores will fall
into a favorable spot and grow or germinate.

Among the more complex animals and plants, the usual means
of reproduction is by the union of egg and sperm. Each
contains half a life, in effect, neither egg nor sperm is able to
develop without the other. The combination of egg and sperm,
however, gives hereditary results different from those produced
by fission or budding, where the new cells are almost like those
of the parent. An animal created by sexual reproduction must
be slightly different than either of its parents, since it inherits
part of its make-up from each. The different offspring of such
a union may vary significantly from one another. Some may be
hardier, more suited to changing conditions and thus better
able to survive. This process of evolution by natural selection
has populated the world with a great variety of interesting
creatures, each adapted to its special place in the sun.

COMMON OBJECTS
SEEN THROUGH
AN EARLY MICROSCOPE

1 Frog's skin

2 Human blood cells with white corpuscle

3 Blood cell of the pigeon

4 Blood cell of the Proteus anguinus (an eel-shaped amphibian)

5 Blood cell of the tortoise

6 Blood cell of the frog, showing projecting nucleus

7 Blood cell of the roach (a fresh-water fish)

8 Human nail

9 Cross section of human thigh bone

10 White connective tissue

11 Cells on surface of the tongue

12 Peacock feather

13 Cross section of hedgehog spine

14 Sheep ligament

15 Epithelial cells of the human nose, showing cilia

16 Ostrich leg bone

17 Canary feather

18 Duck feather, showing interlocking barbules

19 Blood circulation in frog's foot (dark spots caused by pigment)

20 Sparrow feather

21 Feather of a chicken's tail

22 Fiber cells in crystalline lens of a fish's eye

23 Nerve cell and insulating sheath

24 Striated muscle fiber

25 Cross section of a tooth

26 Longitudinal section of a tooth

27 Sweat duct in the human finger

28 Cartilage cells in the eyecup of the haddock

29 Cells of the palate teeth of the ray (a salt-water fish)

30 Cross section of pig's rib, showing bone and cartilage cells (top)

31 Pigment in the eye

32 Pigment in the bat's wing

33 Pigment in a prawn shell

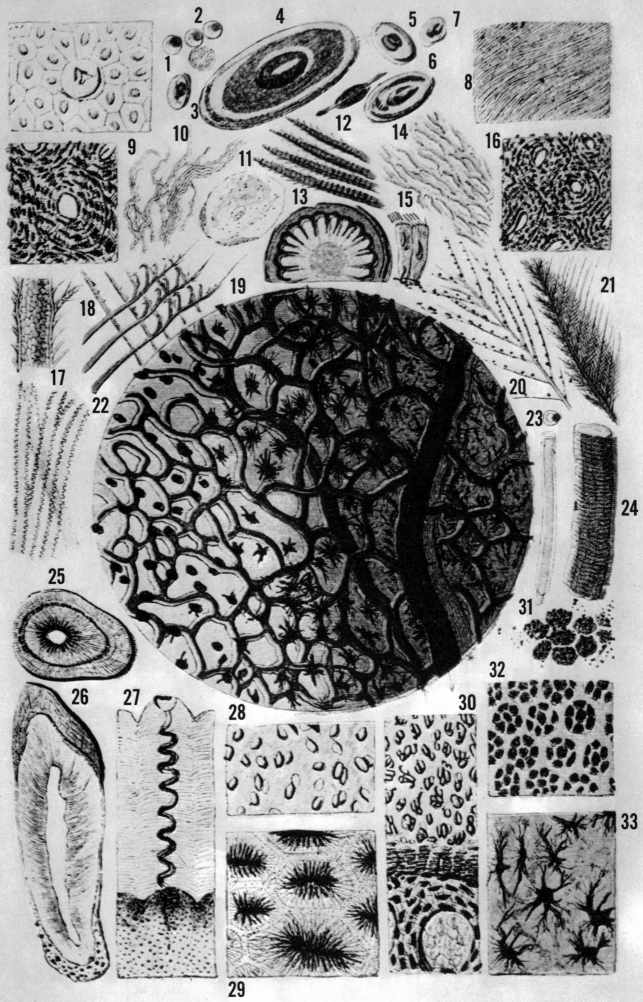

HOW THE MICROSCOPE WORKS

Before we begin our tour of the world under the microscope let us see how this marvelous instrument is constructed. The basic microscope has three parts: a tube, which holds the lenses in the proper relation to each other; a body, which supports the tube; and a platform, or stage, beneath the tube. The object one wishes to see, usually mounted on a glass slide to protect it because of its small size, rests on the stage. Clear focusing is provided by coarse and fine adjusting screws. They bring the lens into the exact position where the tiny object on the stage can be seen most clearly.

The lenses, of course, are the heart of the microscope. The instruments in common use in laboratories, high schools, and universities usually have lenses with a magnification limit of four hundred or five hundred times its original size. (Magnification can also be given as, four hundred diameters, four hundred power, or 400X.) Each microscope of this type has two kinds of lenses—the objective lens located near the stage, which magnifies the object, and the ocular lens near the top of the tube, which enlarges the image produced by the objective lens. Actually, neither is a single lens; each is made of several closely fitted lenses, all working together in the optical system.

To find the total magnification provided by the two-lens system, multiply the power of the objective lens by the power of the ocular lens. For example, if a microscope has an objective lens of ten diameters and an ocular lens of five diameters, the total magnification will be fifty diameters (50X). By changing the objective or ocular lens, a variety of magnifications can be used with specimens of various sizes. Today, most microscopes have revolving nosepieces which have two or three objective lenses attached. These are easily rotated to give the desired magnification power.

Like every man-made device, the microscope has limitations. Only objects which can transmit or reflect a good deal of light can be seen under the microscope, since the light rays are spread out and lose a good deal of their strength when they pass through the lens system. But a great number of objects can be placed under microscopic study.

Through the years, scientists have learned the best ways to prepare materials for examination, and many new objects have come into the microscope's range. If the object to be viewed is a liquid, a very thin layer, called a smear, may be placed on a slide. Some objects are thin enough or small enough to be looked at as a whole mount— the tiny microbes in a drop of water, for example, can be viewed live and whole. But most materials are not small enough to be looked at like this. In order to see the internal structures of some objects, such as the stems of plants, the materials are cut into very thin slices called sections. To prepare a section, the material is soaked in paraffin and shaped into blocks which are then sliced on a machine like a meat slicer, called a microtome. It can cut sections that are only 1/250 of an inch thick. Some of the materials photographed in this book are living whole mounts; others are cross sections or longitudinal sections.

To take the photographs presented in this book on the microscopic world, the author used a special reflex-viewing camera. This camera allows the specimens to be seen through the lenses of the microscope, rather than through a camera lens. This eliminates focusing the camera and framing the object on the slide, problems which are critical when working with such tiny specimens. The camera has a bellows attachment to keep unwanted light off the photographic negative. The bellows is attached to the microscope tube, since the lens system of the microscope takes the place of the camera lens.

A transformer boosts the normal power of illumination and allows shorter film exposure. This is necessary with the use of high-power lenses, since less and less light is transmitted through the lens system as magnification increases. A color-correction filter changes the artificial light to natural color for photographic work. However, an object is often stained with an artificial color to bring out particular details.

Now it is time to enter the fascinating world of the micro-universe, to see the living creatures that live below the threshold of natural human vision. We shall look into the heart of living matter and discover the processes of life itself. Our adventure into the microscopic world begins.

RADIOLARIA: WONDERS OF THE SEA

The sea is home to thousands of fascinating creatures, ranging in size from huge whales and giant squid to animals too small for human eyes to see. The existence of such tiny organisms as we see in this first picture was unsuspected until the microscope extended man's vision. Now we know that microscopic forms of life make up by far the greatest number of living things in the sea and on land as well.

It is from this almost unbelievable number of tiny sea forms that we have taken our first subjects for examination under the microscope. These are the skeletons of little animals called Radiolaria *(ray-dee-oh-LAY-ree-uh)*. There are a great many different kinds of Radiolaria, some of which are among the most beautiful living things found on earth. The skeletons of ten varieties appear here.

Radiolaria make up one part of an immense number of microscopic organisms in the sea. These tiny, drifting forms, which have neither legs for crawling on the ocean floor nor fins to help them swim, are called plankton, from a Greek word which means "wandering." There are both plant and animal plankton, most of them microscopic in size. Plankton are found in vast quantities in the surface waters of all the oceans of the globe. The existence of all marine life depends on such creatures, helplessly drifting before the wind and the currents that drive the sea. For plankton is the basis of the oceanic food chain, and is often called "the grass of the sea."

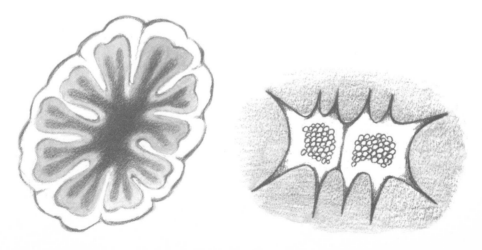

A detailed drawing of some of the one-celled forms of plankton found in the sea.

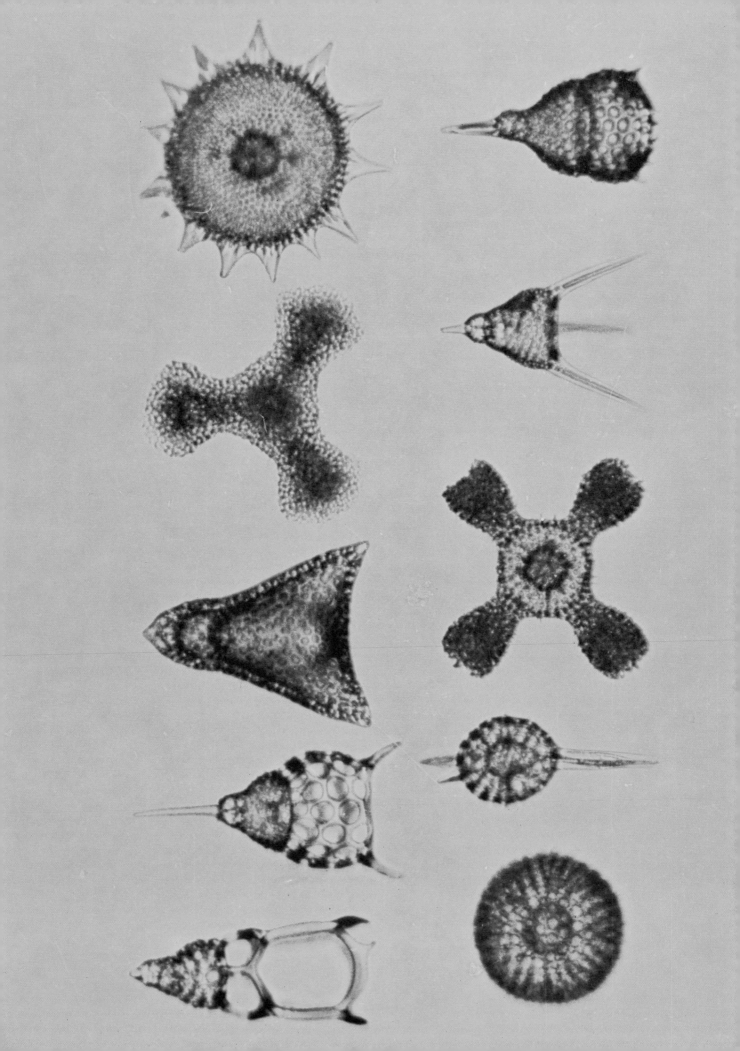

FIRST LIFE ON EARTH

Here is a closer view of one of the radiolarian skeletons in the first picture. This tiny animal feeds on plant forms of plankton, which manufacture their own food from sunlight. Both plant and animal plankton serve as food for a multitude of small sea creatures. In fact, nine-tenths of all food consumed by sea life is plankton! It is eaten by small fish, turtles, jellyfish, barnacles, shrimp, sponges, and many other kinds of small animals. Some of these, such as fish and shrimp, are in turn eaten by larger fish, which are food for still larger sea life. And so the chain goes. Curiously, the largest creatures of the sea, the giant blue whales, which are sometimes more than eighty feet long, feed on plankton, too. The whales have special "combs" in their mouths which trap the microscopic creatures.

Life began in the sea many millions of years ago, and the first living forms were probably similar to the tiny Radiolaria, so widespread today. When these creatures die, their skeletons, composed of silica or chalky calcium carbonate, drift slowly to the bottom of the sea. Year after year, century after century, the ocean bottom has been showered with a gentle rain of skeletons. Today they cover two million square miles of ocean floor, an area known as the "radiolarian ooze." Radiolaria fossils are also found in many large deposits on land. The chalk cliffs of Dover, England are layers of billions on billions of plankton skeletons deposited when the land was under the sea.

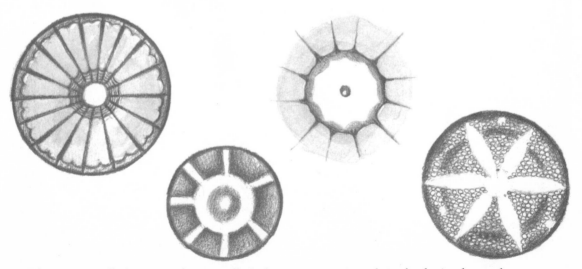

These one-celled water plants, called diatoms, are found in both fresh- and salt-water.

DIDINIA DEVOURING PARAMECIA

The long, slipper-shaped animals shown here are single-celled paramecia (*pair-ah-MEE-shee-uh*). The paramecium is probably one of the first animals Leeuwenhoek saw in his simple microscope. These creatures live in fresh water throughout the world. Their bodies are covered with tiny hairs which beat in waves and propel them in swift spirals through the water. The paramecium was one of the first animals in the evolutionary series to have a rigid outer surface. Thus, unlike its cousin the amoeba, it has a definite shape and a distinct back and front.

Two of the paramecia in this picture did not swim fast enough to escape the didinia (*dih-DIN-ee-uh*) shown feeding on them. Didinia are carnivorous (meat-eating) creatures which eat almost nothing but paramecia. They hook onto their victims with a sort of snout, then swallow them whole. A much higher form of animal—the snake—consumes its food in the same way. A didinium doubles in size when it has swallowed a paramecium, but in a few hours it will have digested one meal and will be ready for another.

In the sea or on land, the microscopic single-celled animals are the most numerous animal group. One-celled animals are called protozoa. There are thousands of varieties of protozoa, and they live in all sorts of places—in the waters of ocean, lake, and stream, in the soil, in hot deserts and cold arctic regions, and even inside other animals. Although they are microscopic in size and are made up of only one cell, these creatures can and must carry on all the basic functions of life: breathing, moving about in search of food, feeding, resting, and reproducing their own kind. These activities are common to all living things.

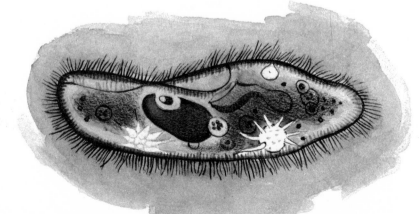

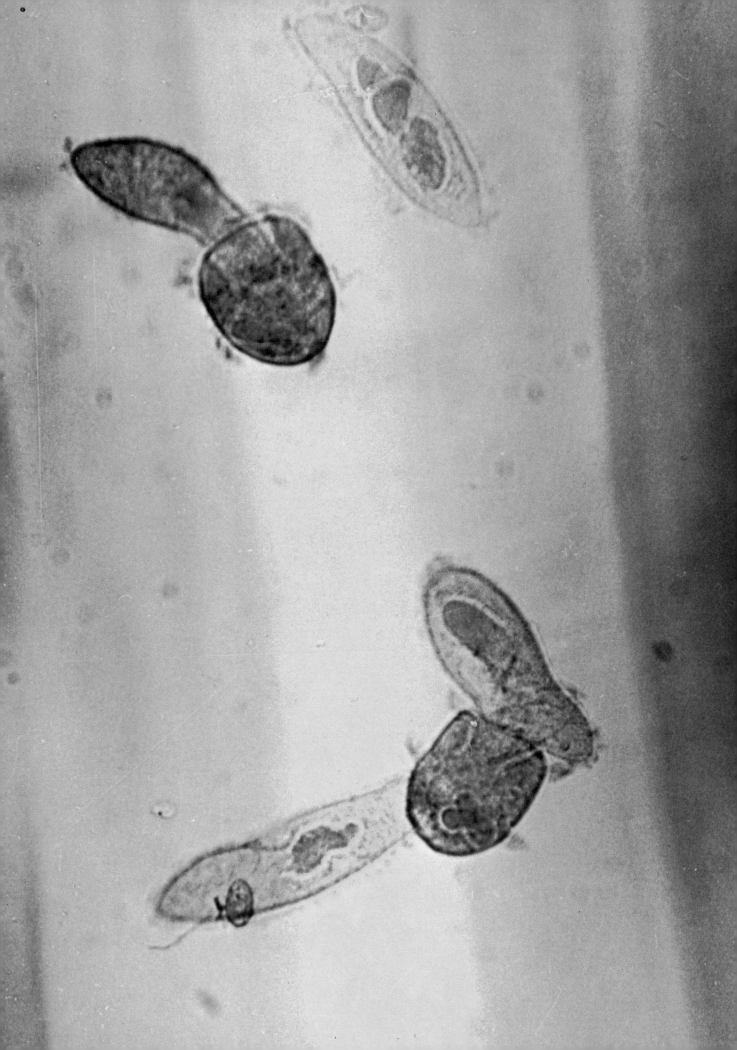

VOLVOX: COLONY OF PROTOZOA

This is another type of protozoa. It is quite different from those we have just seen. Volvox *(VOHL-voks)* is a colony of thousands of one-celled individuals set firmly in a hollow sphere of jelly. Each cell could live independently, but in a colony a few of them have become slightly specialized for certain functions. For instance, each cell on the surface of the ball has two threadlike projections which strike the water like whips to move the colony through the water. These "oars" work together so that the ball can roll along, stop, or even reverse its direction. A few of the Volvox cells have the ability to divide and form new "daughter" cells. Each daughter cell divides many times until it is a tiny Volvox colony, resting inside the hollow ball of the mother colony, with all its whiplike projections turned inward. When the daughter colony becomes full-grown the mother colony breaks open. The daughter turns her oars outward, whirling away to search for food. Then she in turn becomes the mother to new colonies.

Some biologists do not believe that the Volvox is an animal. They think it should be classified as a plant. For, while it does move about and feed like an animal, it also makes some of its own food from chlorophyll. This green pigment is essential to the food-making process in plants, called photosynthesis, which uses the energy of sunlight to build up carbohydrates from carbon dioxide, minerals, and water.

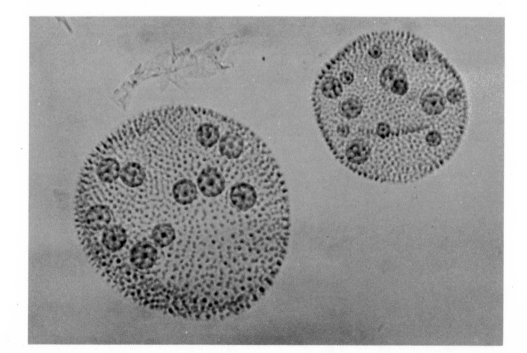

SPIROGYRA: RIBBONS OF CHLOROPHYLL

Here is another colony of single-celled organisms. These are definitely plants. The cells of this colony of spirogyra are connected end to end, rather than in a ball like the Volvox. The dark spiral bands seen in these specimens are ribbons of chlorophyll, which are bright green in the living plant. Spirogyra is usually seen as a slimy green scum on the surfaces of ponds, but under the microscope the individual strands become delicately beautiful.

Spirogyra belongs to a group of plants called algae (*AL-jee*), which are found in every kind of body of water on earth—pond, lake, stream, river, and ocean. They are truly plants, but they are as unlike the grass or rosebush in our backyard as Volvox is unlike man. Algae have no roots, stem, leaves, or flowers. But they do have chlorophyll, which enables them to manufacture their own food, just as the grass and rosebush do.

Most kinds of algae live in water, but they can also be found in soil, on rocks and fence posts, on tree bark, and even in snow and ice. The Red Sea is named for a red algae which occurs in vast numbers in its waters. The seaweeds common on the Atlantic and Pacific shores are examples of very large types of algae.

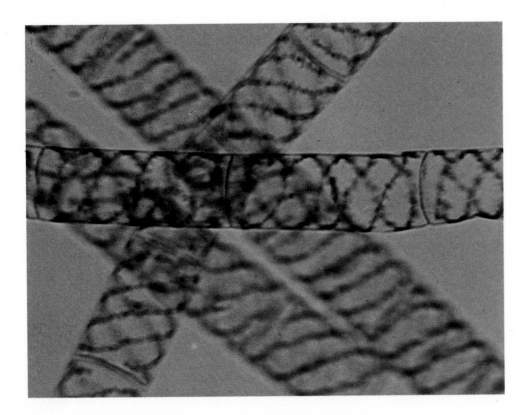

FUCUS: COMPLEX SEA PLANT

In this picture we see our first cross section, taken from the ribbonlike body of another algae, a sea plant called fucus (*FEW-kus*), or rockweed. It is found in shallow coastal waters, attached to the rocks by suction disks called "holdfasts" at the base of the plant.

Fucus, unlike the simpler spirogyra, contains different types of cells. Each type is dependent upon the others, and each performs special functions. The dark, thin line around the outside of this fucus "leaf" section is a tough layer of cells, which protect the plant. Just inside this layer is a thicker group of cortex cells, where the process of photosynthesis takes place. In the center is an area of loosely connected cells which form the conductive tissues, through which water and food materials flow. The round, bubblelike cavities hugging the outer walls of the plant are conceptacles, which contain the reproductive organs. This relatively simple plant is nevertheless bisexual and reproduces by the union of egg and sperm cells. The small dark spots in the conceptacles are the female reproductive organs; the sperm cells develop separately. Within each of these dark spots there are eight eggs. When the eggs are mature they are released through openings in the conceptacles and the outer layer. In the picture, eggs are spewing forth from three of the conceptacles. Fertilization may occur when active sperm cells, released from other conceptacles, unite with the eggs.

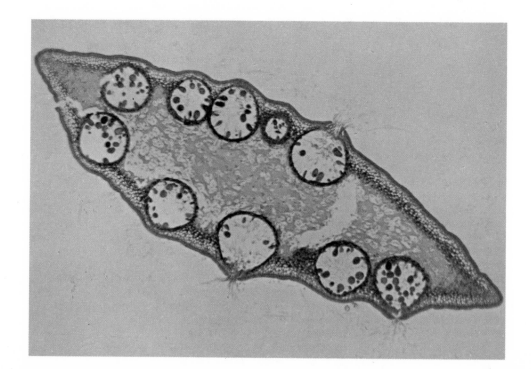

MOSS: WORLD-WIDE GREEN

Mosses, the tiny green plants found all over the world, are the second of the great plant groups. They are not particularly specialized and are able to survive conditions of cold or drought which often kill larger, more complex plants.

This picture shows a longitudinal section of one very special part of a moss. The long hairlike cells on each side appear, in the unsectioned plant, to be leaves. But mosses do not have leaves. These "leafy" parts are protective coverings for the sexual organs of the moss. Each plant has both male and female reproductive organs. The male organs are called antheridia (an-thur-ID-ee-uh). The oval, sperm-bearing antheridia, stained a deep green in this picture, lie within the protecting "leaves." The brown-stained cells between the antheridia are hairs, apparently without function.

Mosses multiply in several ways. All of them can regenerate. Almost any small bit of moss can produce a whole, new plant. Some species have special reproductive buds called "brood bodies." But most interesting of all is the alternation of sexual and asexual generations which all mosses go through. Minute spores produced by the plant in its asexual stage become the familiar leafy structures which carpet the forest floor. Male antheridia grow at the tips of some of these "leaves," female organs at others. Only a drop of rain or a film of morning dew is necessary for the sperm produced in the antheridia to swim to the eggs within the female parts of the moss. Then a new spore-bearing plant will be produced by the union of egg and sperm, and the cycle of alternating generations will begin again.

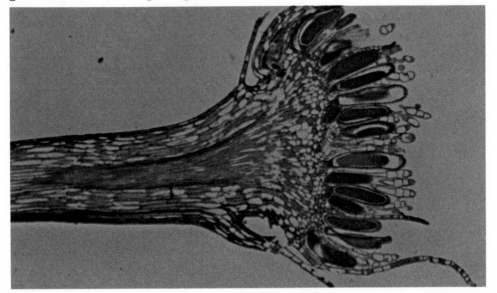

ROOT TIP: ARMORED GROWTH

Most of the plants around us belong to the largest of the great plant groups—the seed-bearing plants. There are three basic parts found in all seed plants. These are: the roots, which anchor the plant to the ground and absorb water and minerals from the soil; the stems, which support the plant, provide transportation channels between roots and leaves, and store food; and the leaves, which, with the aid of sunlight manufacture food from the water and minerals absorbed by the roots.

The first part to develop after a seed has sprouted is the root. In their search for water and food, some roots may grow several feet long before the plant appears above ground. The length of a root increases only at its tip. In order to protect this vital part, each root tip has large, tough cells which form the root cap. Behind this cap are rapidly dividing cells, which replace the old cap as it is worn away by friction.

Next there is a section in which cells grow longer, extending the root into the soil. These longer cells begin to differ in size and shape according to the jobs they will perform in the mature plant. Some become "skin" cells to protect the root; others form vascular tubes through which water and food pass. Some form storage tissues, and still others form root hairs, which carry on the actual absorption of water from behind the root cap.

Roots may be of several different types. Some plants, like the dandelion, have a very thick main taproot which reaches far down into the earth for water and minerals. Carrots and beets have short taproots which store lots of food. Grasses and corn have masses of branching roots which remain close to the surface.

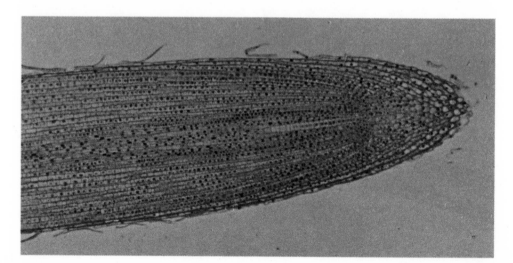

MATURE OAK ROOT

This cross section of an oak root was taken some distance from the tip. It shows how the root structure has changed in a mature root. The outer layer is made of thick skin cells and is similar to the bark of a stem. Just beneath the outer layer is a growth layer, stained red, from which branch roots develop. Beneath that is a green layer of food-carrying tissues, and within that, another green layer which carries water. The tissues in an oak root grow in much the same way as those in the woody stem. In old roots, you can sometimes even distinguish annual rings, although they are never so pronounced as they are in the trunk, where they indicate the age of the tree.

Some plants have prop roots, which grow out of the stem above ground and help support the plant. Because of its shallow root system, corn has prop roots. Swamp trees, such as banyan and cypress, sometimes have prop roots as large as their trunks. Some climbing plants, like the ivies, develop roots along the stem which help them cling to walls and tree trunks. And several tropical orchids that grow on the branches of trees have aerial roots that never enter the soil at all. These unattached roots have a spongy outer layer which absorbs moisture from the humid tropical climates.

CEDAR CELLS

Scientists first looked into the micro-world because they wanted to understand the physical nature of life, but in the process they overlooked other parts of the world around them—the very chairs they sat on, for example. Here, we see a section of wood from a cedar tree. All that remains of this once-living material is the rigid walls of the cells.

In early spring, when water is plentiful and growth is rapid, the wood cells of a tree are quite large. But as water becomes scarce in summer, growth slows down and the cells developing then are smaller and smaller, until cell growth stops entirely at the end of summer. In this picture you can see the difference between the large cells that grew in spring and the smaller cells of late summer. It is this seasonal difference in cell growth that produces annual rings and enables botanists to estimate the age of a tree.

Rings of a living tree are examined by taking a coring near the base of the tree. By noting the thickness of the rings, one can tell the years of little and abundant rainfall. In fact, a skilled "reader" looking at the coring of an old tree can tell what the weather was like in that area hundreds of years ago. The rings of very old trees are often of vital importance. When archaeologists examined the former home of the Mesa Verde Indians in Colorado, they learned that this flourishing tribe had suddenly and mysteriously abandoned their cliff dwellings sometime after the year 1276. The mystery was solved when corings of old local trees showed signs of severe drought which began during that year.

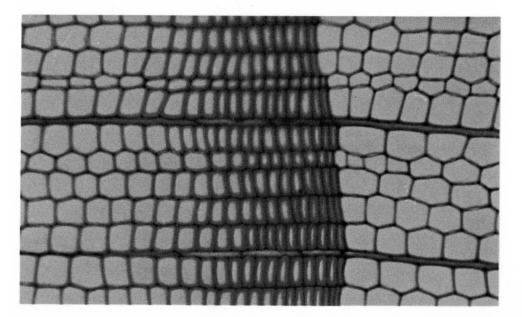

LEAF: NETWORK OF VEINS

A leaf is perhaps the simplest part of any plant. Here we see a leaf after the delicate green tissue has died, and only the skeletal network of veins is left. When the leaf was alive, the veins were embedded in the soft, thin tissue. They supported the tissue, which manufactures food from sunlight. They brought raw materials to leaf cells and carried photosynthesized food from the leaf to the body of the plant.

Leaves show two main types of vein patterns—parallel and netted. In parallel structure, found in grasses, corn leaves, the leaves of daffodils and other plants, the veins run in straight, vertical lines. In netted structure—as in the leaf shown here—the veins form an interlocking pattern, running in all directions. The leaves of most of our common flowers and trees have this interlocking pattern.

For animal life, leaves are very important. They not only produce the oxygen necessary for living things, but are themselves the basic food, directly or indirectly, of all land animals. For every animal must either eat plants or consume other animals which themselves are dependent upon plants for food.

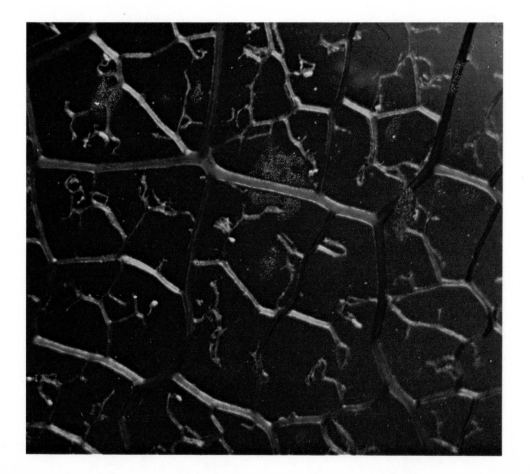

PINE NEEDLE: STREAMLINED LEAF

Not all leaves are thin, flat sheets of tissue. Pine needles are also leaves. Their surfaces are reduced for survival in dry climates, since a leaf with a large surface area would lose too much water through evaporation. But pine leaves have kept their ability to use the energy of sunlight to make food. They contain the same chlorophyll found in flat leaves. Here we see a cross section of a ponderosa pine needle.

The ponderosa is a "two-needle" type of pine. That is, its leaves come in bundles of two. Other pines are three-needle, four-needle, or five-needle types. The layer of dark cells around the outside of the needle is the epidermis, or skin. These cells are very thick and water-resistant. Their job is to protect the leaf and prevent excessive loss of water. In the evergreens of the northern climates, water loss may occur in winter when the surface soil is frozen, and water is unavailable to plants. Broad-leaved plants solve this problem by dropping their leaves in winter and stopping their growth. They become dormant.

Just beneath the epidermis a light-colored layer of chlorophyll-bearing cells can be seen. Here the plant cells transform solar energy into living material. In the center of the needle is the structure which corresponds to the veins of flat leaves. It is called the vascular cylinder. This part performs the same transportation function that veins do. This vascular cylinder is surrounded by a chain of cells called the endoderm, or "inner skin," which looks like a white necklace in this picture. The empty circles near the corners of the needle are resin ducts which ooze a sticky pitch whenever a needle has been damaged. It is this resin which gives evergreens their familiar "piny" smell.

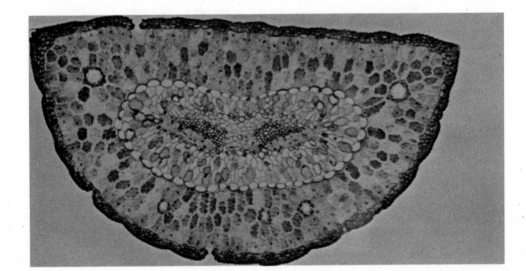

STEM: PIPELINES FOR FOOD S 1709853

This is a cross-section view of the stem of a young clover plant. Young stems usually have three distinct parts: bark, transporting tissues, and pith. At the center of this stem is the pith, the pulplike material which supports the plant. Pith cells are large and thin-walled. Outside the pith is a ring of vascular bundles, or conducting tissues. These are the pipelines that carry water and minerals up out of the ground and transport manufactured food down to the body of the plant. One side, called xylem (*ZIGH-lem*), and visible in this picture as the rows of cells pointing toward the center of the stem, carries the water and minerals; the other side, called phloem (*FLOW-em*), carries the food. Thus, besides supporting the plant, the stem is also the connecting line between roots and leaves.

Between xylem and phloem is the green growth, or cambium (*KAM-bee-um*), layer. New cells of all kinds are produced here as the plant grows. Annual plants such as corn, however, have no cambium layer, since the next year's growth comes from a new seed.

Stems may be of many sizes and shapes, from the trunks of giant redwood trees to the extremely short stems of dandelion plants. Some vines have stems no thicker than a thread, and some plants grow so close to the ground that one can hardly speak of a stem at all. Although stems differ a great deal in appearance, their internal structure is pretty much the same in all plants. But stem structure varies considerably with the age of the plant.

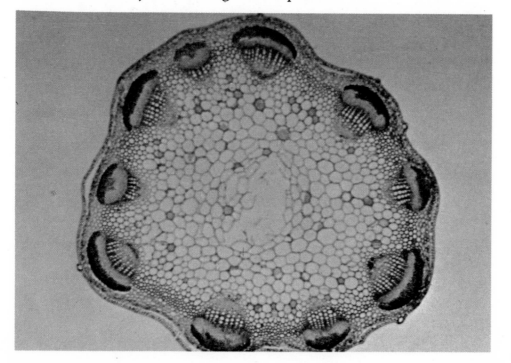

GROWTH OF A STEM

As stems get older, great changes take place. The thin, living skin of the young stem is gradually replaced by a thick, protective bark. Bark is not a living tissue, and new layers must be added each season as the old bark is split by the growing tree. Just beneath the bark is a layer called the bark cambium, which forms a cylinder around the living tree.

As the plant ages, the transporting tissues enlarge to keep up with the growing tree until the entire center of the stem may be taken up almost entirely by xylem and phloem. The remaining pith sometimes extends from the center in rays. Excess food is stored in these rays. In this section from a flower-bearing vine called Dutchman's-pipe we can see the rays are very large.

The phloem tubes form a layer of cells beneath the bark cambium. The xylem grows rapidly, becoming sapwood. Great quantities of water are carried by the sapwood, which often takes up the major part of the stem or trunk. Between the xylem and the wood is a second layer of cambium, a growth layer that produces xylem on the outside and sapwood on the inside. The cambium layers are usually too small to be seen in a tree without the aid of a microscope. They stand out clearly in this tiny stem only because they were stained dark during the preparation of the micro-slide. The inner cambium layer is perhaps the most important part of the tree. It is here that the growth in circumference of the stem and branches takes place.

Annual rings of growth are formed by the alternately rapid and slow production of cells by the cambium layer during spring and summer. This stem has eight annual rings and is thus eight years old.

MATURE STEM

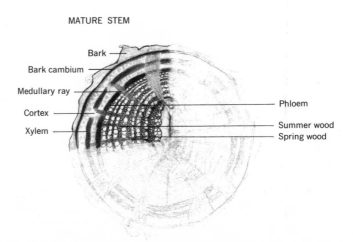

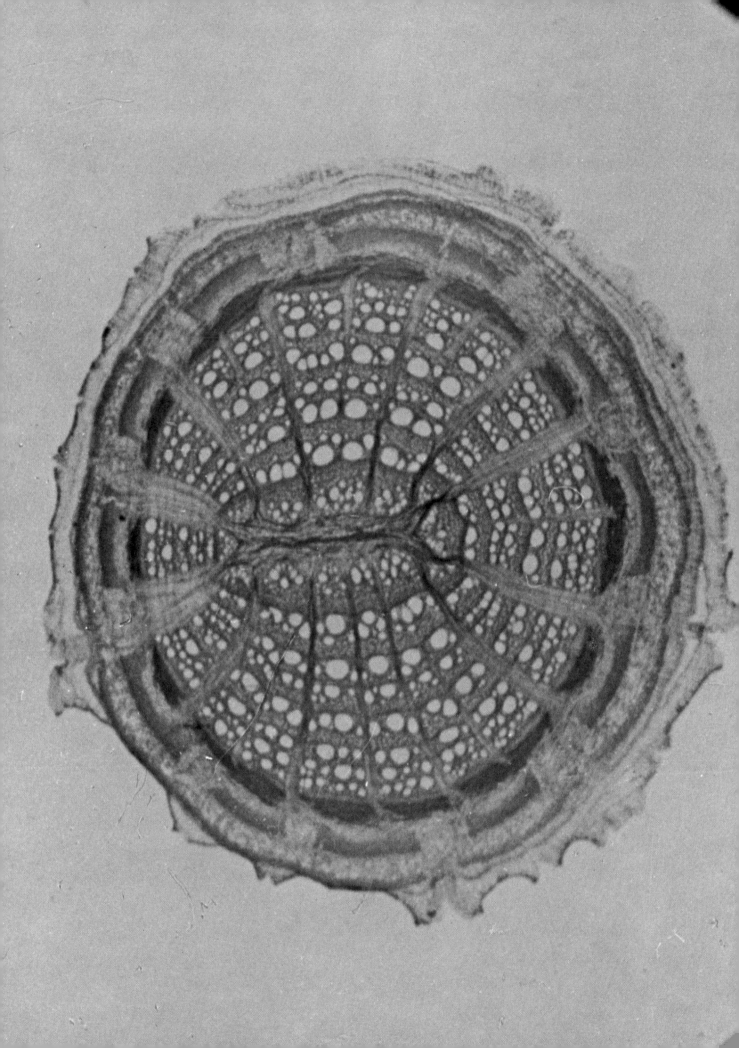

PRUNE BUD: WAITING FOR SPRING

A'nother important part of seed-bearing plants is the buds, from which nature produces its endless display of flowers. In some plants, each bud contains both the leaf and flower parts. In others, flower and leaf buds are separate. Sometimes the buds are protected by special scale leaves. These are much thicker than green leaves and are used to protect the buds from drying out. Our picture shows the thick, dark scale leaves encircling the leaf and flower bud of a tree belonging to the prune family. Beneath the scale leaves are the folded immature leaves, and in the center are two clusters of flowers ready to burst into bloom.

With the coming of spring there is a great burst of green all over the world. The scale leaves suddenly unfold, and tiny green leaves shoot forth and grow rapidly to full size. The change happens suddenly because the leaves have been there all the time, tightly folded during winter, waiting for the warmth of sunlight to signal spring.

Below the bud in this picture is a dark abscission (*ab-SIZ-un*) layer at the base of last year's leaf. When winter comes, these abscission layers pinch off the flow of water to the leaves, so that no water can evaporate from the leaves during the dormant period. Usually the leaves drop off when this occurs.

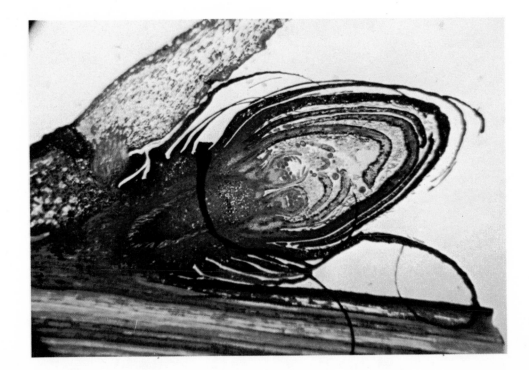

FLOWER BUD: STOREHOUSE OF LIFE

Quite aside from their beauty, flowers perform a vital function in plant life—the production of fertile seeds for the next generation of plants. It is in the flowers of a plant that the sex organs are contained. Sometimes male and female organs are in one flower, as in this prune bud. Sometimes they are in separate flowers. Male organs produce pollen grains, and female organs produce seeds.

During the winter, flowers rest tightly folded in buds along the branches of trees and shrubs. The delicate green structures folded over the bud in this picture are the petals. The large structure in the middle is the pistil. The seeds lie in the ovary at the base of the pistil. The speckled spheres within the flower are the folded and dormant pollen-bearing parts of the flower, called stamens (*STAY-mens*). Each speck is a grain of pollen. There may be many thousands of such grains within each flower, and their numbers increase the chances of fertilization.

If both pollen and seeds are produced in the same flower, as in this prune bud, the pollen-producing stamens usually grow above the pistil so that ripe pollen floats down to the seeds. When spring comes, the petals unfold, the stamens rise on slender stalks, and pollen is released. The end of the pistil is sticky, to make the pollen grains cling to it. These grains will travel down the stalk of the pistil into the ovary, where fertilization, or pollinization, takes place.

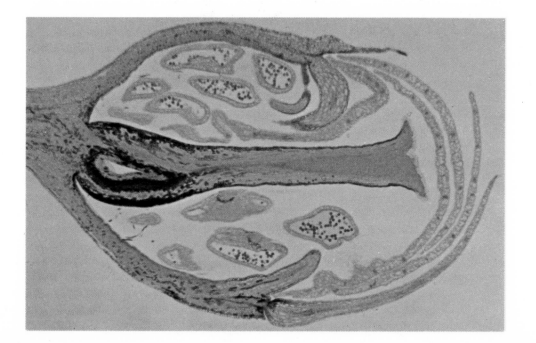

BUTTERNUT SEEDS

After pollinization, the petals of a flower wilt and fall off. The fertilized seed begins to divide and grow within the ovary. Soon specialization begins: some cells form protective tissues for the seed; some store food for the seed until its roots can function; and others form the first roots and tiny leaves. When this process of growth is finished, the seed is ripe. It will drop to the ground, and grow into a new plant if conditions are favorable.

To most people the word fruit means such things as apples, pears, or oranges. But to the botanist, fruit indicates any seed with an enlarged, ripened ovary surrounding it. Some fruits are soft and fleshy, like peaches and tomatoes. Others are dry, like the butternut in this picture. The thick, hard outer covering protects the central seed and the food packed around it.

Botanists talk about three types of fruit. Simple fruits are those that develop from a single ovary, such as peaches, olives, pears, and cranberries. Each ovary, however, may contain a great many seeds— as the watermelon, for instance. Fruits, such as the raspberry and blackberry, are aggregate fruits. They develop from several separate ovaries contained in a single flower. Each little bump on a raspberry is actually an ovary and contains seeds. Multiple fruits are those which develop from any flowers united in one structure, such as pineapples, mulberries, or figs. Each bump on a pineapple is a single flower, and its core is actually the stem around which the flowers grew.

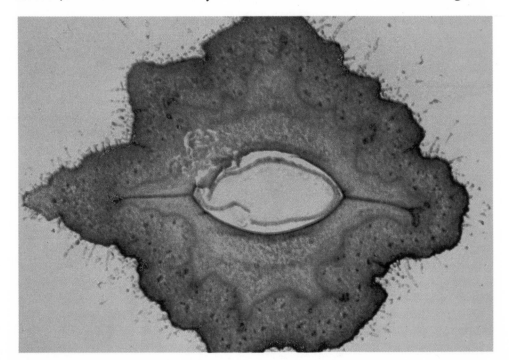

BASSWOOD SEEDS

Here are two cross sections of the fleshy fruit of a basswood tree, in which the seeds are protected by a soft, pulpy material. A number of ovaries can be seen around the core. Only those seeds which have been pollinated within the ovaries can develop.

Fruits such as the lemon and apple drop to the ground when the seeds are ripe, and if moisture and temperature conditions are good, the seeds sprout. Thus we often find a tree with a cluster of young plants around its base, where the fruit has dropped. Lighter seeds, such as the milkweed and dandelion, have "parachutes" which enable them to be carried a great distance by the wind. Others, like the maple and linden, have "wings" to ride the wind currents. There are plants whose seeds have barbs or hooks, and depend upon passing animals for travel. Some seeds have sticky coverings that get tangled in animal fur. If we walk across fields in summer, we are likely to return with shoes and socks covered with sticktights and cockleburs.

When animals or birds eat fruits, the seeds may pass through the animal undigested and be deposited hundreds of miles from where they were picked up. Under telephone wires or along fences where birds have gathered, one can usually find a great variety of plants which have sprouted from such seeds. A few plants, such as the coconut palm, which grows on islands in the Pacific, depend on water to scatter their seeds. The palms grow along the shores of the islands, often leaning over the water. The nuts drop into the water and may be carried great distances by ocean currents.

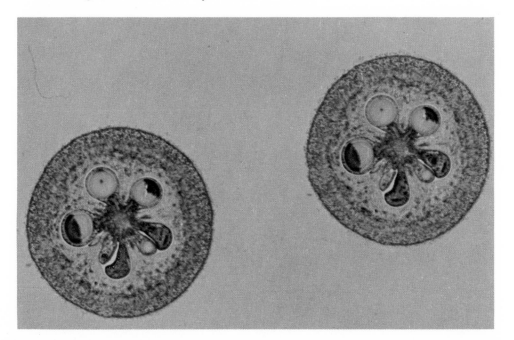

MIRACLE OF THE SEED

Each ripe seed contains within its protective shell the astonishing potential for becoming a new plant. Seeds may be ready to sprout as soon as they are released from the parent plant, or they may need a period of rest or even freezing weather before they can grow.

This picture shows a lily seed ready for germination, or sprouting. The green structure surrounding the seed is the protective seed coat. The circle in the center is the plant which will develop into a young seedling. The darker materials around the plant are stored food. The seedling will live on this food while roots and leaves are developing.

All seeds need great amounts of water before they can germinate. They also need oxygen. If seeds are buried too deeply in the soil, they will remain dormant (not growing). Seed development is also controlled by temperature. In arctic regions seeds are able to sprout at temperatures which would kill tropical plants.

Willow and poplar seeds must find the right conditions for sprouting within a few days or they will die. The acorns of some oaks will not sprout after one year. But some seeds can remain dormant for years, some perhaps for centuries, without losing their ability to grow. Wheat kernels will sprout after ten years; tobacco seeds remain alive for twenty years, and cottonseeds for twenty-five years. There are reports of seeds, found in jars three thousand years old, that sprouted when given proper growing conditions!

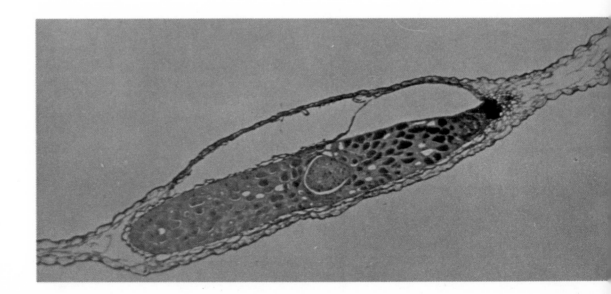

PINE CONE: PATIENT SEEDS

The pine tree is not a flowering plant, but it must produce seeds in its closed cones so that future generations may grow. Pine cones may be either male or female, just like flowers. The cones which most of us notice are the large female cones. Male cones are much smaller —usually less than an inch long—and often go unnoticed unless you look closely at the branches of the tree.

This picture shows a female cone cut into a longitudinal section. In each scale, near the central stalk that it grows from, there is a round ovary. The seeds develop from the ovaries, some of which are visible here. It usually takes two years for a pine cone to mature and release its seeds. The cones of many evergreens fall apart when the seeds ripen. But in some varieties the cones do not open for many years, sometimes not until they decay with age. In some species the cones remain closed until a squirrel breaks them open in search of food. And some cones, such as those of the knobcone pine, may stay closed twenty-five years or more, and then open only when burned by forest fire. Such trees are called "fire-cone" trees.

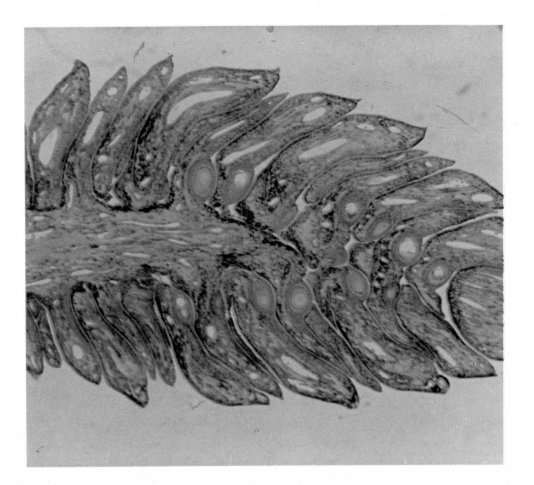

BLOOD CELLS: LIFE'S MAIN STREAM

When Leeuwenhoek began to examine the micro-world through his simple instrument, one of the substances he looked at was blood, the life fluid of all the more complex animals. Through the microscope we can see that blood is not the simple, uniform substance that the naked eye sees. It is composed of several types of cells floating in a liquid medium called plasma. The plasma itself is almost ninety percent water.

This picture shows a smear of the blood cells of a frog. The cells have been stained with a blue dye to bring out the internal structures. The large, dark disk within each cell is the nucleus (*NEW-klee-us*), which could not be seen without the stain.

The blood of an animal contains two main *types* of cells, and each has its special function. The red blood cells carry on the important activity of carrying oxygen from the lungs to all cells of the body so that they can live. If oxygen is cut off, an animal will die in a matter of minutes. The red color of living blood comes from hemoglobin (*HEE-moh-glob-bin*), the important chemical substance that unites easily with oxygen in the lungs. The hemoglobin carries great quantities of oxygen to other body cells, where it is used. The red cells, flowing through the arteries and veins of the circulatory system, also carry food to the body cells.

Blood also contains white cells which destroy disease-producing bacteria. If the skin is broken, the white cells travel to the spot in large numbers and attack any invading bacteria. Without these lifesaving cells, no animal could survive the slightest scratch or the mildest infection.

The electron microscope looks deep into the unbelievably small world beyond even the most powerful light microscope. This scientist can magnify objects up to 200,000 times. By using a fluorescent screen he can obtain a magnification of 500,000 times. Other specially equipped electron microscopes have achieved a magnification power of 2,000,000 times.

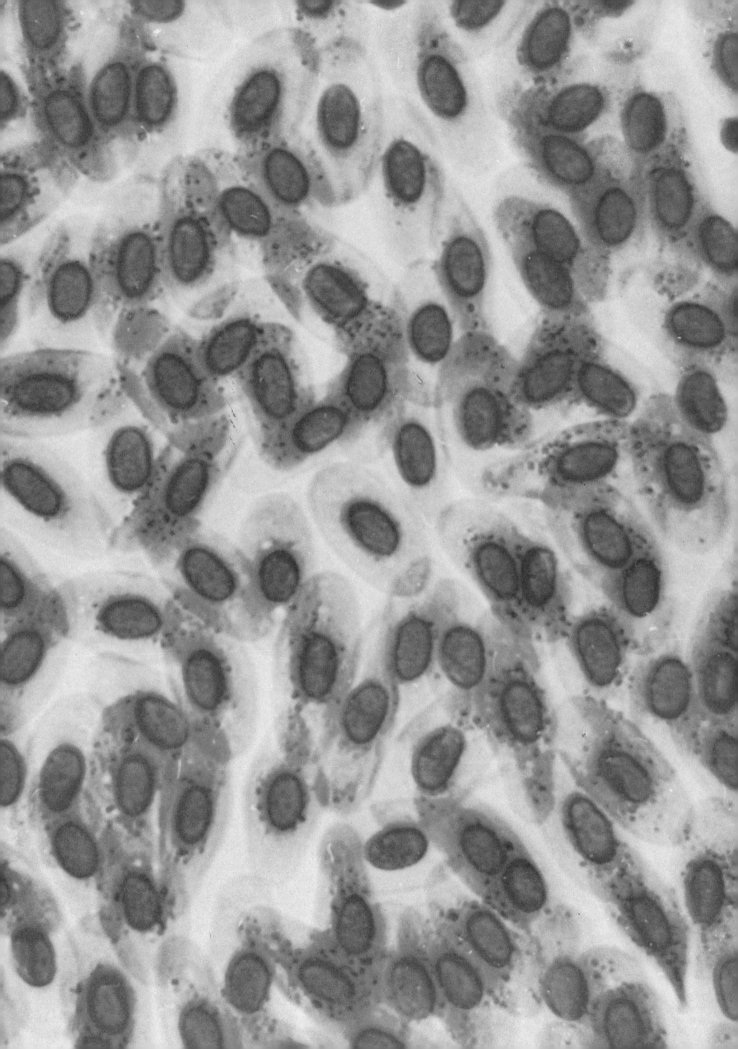

TASTE BUDS OF A RABBIT

This odd-looking, cross section shows taste buds from the tongue of a rabbit. The buds are the bulblike sacs set firmly in the outer layer of the tongue. The inside of each tiny taste bud is lined with numerous nerve cells, which react to substances dissolved in the mouth. Each bud has an opening at the surface of the tongue.

Actually a great deal of what we call tasting is not really tasting at all, but smelling. The two sensations are very closely related, since both are responses to chemical stimuli.

Taste buds help in maintaining a balanced diet by indicating either a good or a flat taste, depending on whether the body needs the food or not. This is why food tastes better after hard work, when the body has used up its stores, and why pregnant mothers may crave certain kinds of foods, as the growing baby uses stored energy at an increased rate.

Although man's taste buds are found only on the tongue, other animals have them outside the mouth as well. Butterflies, for example, have taste buds on their bodies, and some fish even have them on their skin. This lets them test their food before they put it in their mouths.

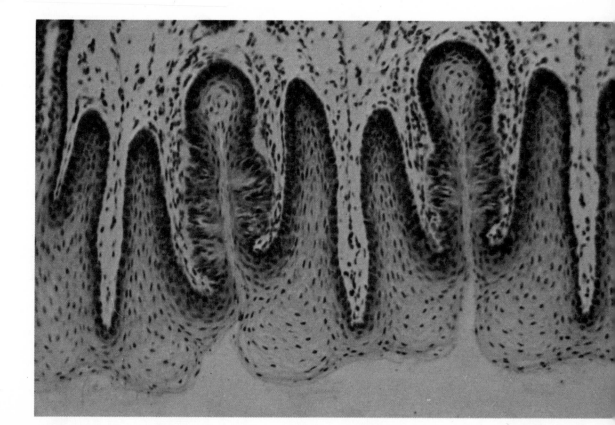

INSECT EYE: OPTICAL HONEYCOMB

Unlike other animals, insects have eyes that cannot be turned or moved. This would seem to be a great handicap, for if an insect cannot see an enemy coming, it is likely to be eaten. But insect eyes have an unusual construction that overcomes this handicap. They have compound eyes. These are made up of a great many single lenses fitted together into one "super eye," looking something like the cells of a honeycomb. Each lens sees part of the image. Scientists think the chief function of the compound eye is to observe movement. Each lens evidently sees the moving object in turn, and a picture of the object and its movement is shown in a sort of mosaic pattern.

The compound eyes of dragonflies and damsel flies are so large that they occupy most of the head. A housefly has about four thousand lenses in its eye. Some ants have only fifty. But the dragonfly may have as many as thirty thousand!

Insects, unlike many animals, do sense color. Flower-visiting species have an especially well-developed color sense. But man sees many more colors than insects do. If you watch bees during the spring and summer, you will see that they are most often attracted by flowers in shades of blue or yellow. On the other hand, butterflies frequently visit bright red and orange flowers.

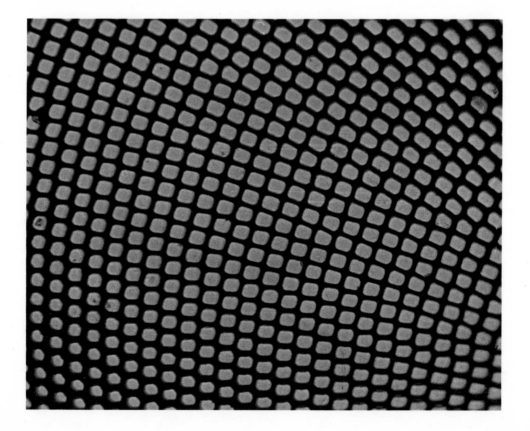

INSIDE A TOOTH

The microscope can be used to examine a great number of objects. Here we see a cross section of a tooth, taken near the root. The inner part, which appears as parallel lines radiating from the center, is dentine, a bonelike material that makes up the bulk of the tooth. Dentine is not as hard as the outer enamel, but it is much harder than bone. Surrounding the dentine is a thin, dark layer of cement which holds the root of the tooth to the jaw. Outside this layer is the enamel, the hardest part of the tooth and one of the most lasting substances in nature. Some animals have unbelievably hard teeth.

Inside the living tooth is an area of soft material called the pulp cavity. The nerves and blood vessels, found here, enter the pulp cavity through the hole in the center of this section. At the base of the tooth there are one or more roots which anchor the tooth to sockets in the jaw.

Only mammals, reptiles, and fish have teeth and can seize and cut the food they eat. Most other animals swallow their food whole. Along with mental development, adaptability, and structures like claws or hoofs and muscular legs, teeth have given mammals their present position of dominance in the world. Teeth are important tools used to catch and hold food. They can also be deadly defense weapons. Both activities are necessary for survival.

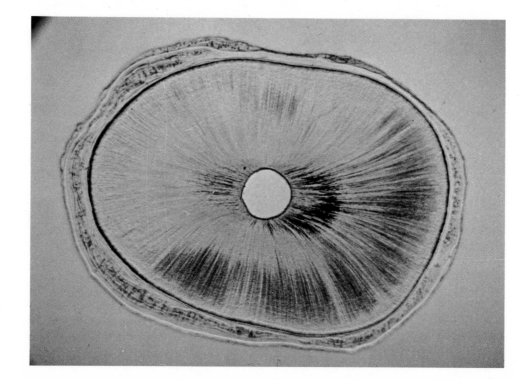

BUTTERFLY SCALES

Summer after summer, butterflies flutter over the gardens of the earth. There are fifty thousand kinds of butterflies in the world, but only some seven hundred fifty of them live in the United States. Most butterflies, certainly the most beautiful, live in the tropics. The largest, with wingspans up to twelve inches, are also tropical.

Butterflies have three pairs of legs and three-part bodies. They belong to an order of insects called Lepidoptera *(lep-ih-DOPP-ter-uh)*, meaning "scaly wings." They are the only insects whose wings are covered with these tiny, overlapping scales, which rub off when you handle a butterfly. This picture shows the scales as they look under the microscope. Actually, the scales are flattened hairs.

The colors of butterflies come from two sources. The reds, browns, and yellows come from pigments or dyes in the scales, set fast while the butterfly is developing in its cocoon. But the metallic colors and the greens and blues of other butterflies are not pigments. The scales on their wings are made of many overlapping layers. These layers act like prisms, breaking up light and scattering it in different directions. This diffraction is the same process that gives sparkling color to a cut diamond or a crystal chandelier.

PLANARIA: RARE REGENERATION

Planaria (*pluh-NAY-ree-uh*) are small flatworms, found in streams all over the world. A small piece of meat placed in quiet waters will often attract hundreds of them in a short time. While you can see planaria with your eye alone, their curious features and abilities come to light only under the microscope.

To begin with, the planaria's mouth is in a most unusual location—in the middle of its body. The mouth opens into an extensive digestive system, with one major branch in front of the mouth and two branches behind. In the picture, the digestive system is stained brown. The mouth, which opens to the rear, can be seen in the center of the planaria's flat, transparent body.

The flatworms were the lowest forms of animal life to develop a definite grouping of sensory organs. Flatworms were also the first to have bilateral symmetry, with one half exactly like the other. All higher forms of life—fish, reptiles, and mammals—have followed suit.

Planaria are widely used in laboratory experiments because of their extraordinary regenerative powers. A planaria that has been cut in two will not die. Each part will regrow its missing half. Within a short time each half will develop into two separate and complete animals. And if the head of a planaria is cut down the center, the little flatworm soon grows two heads joined to one trunk.

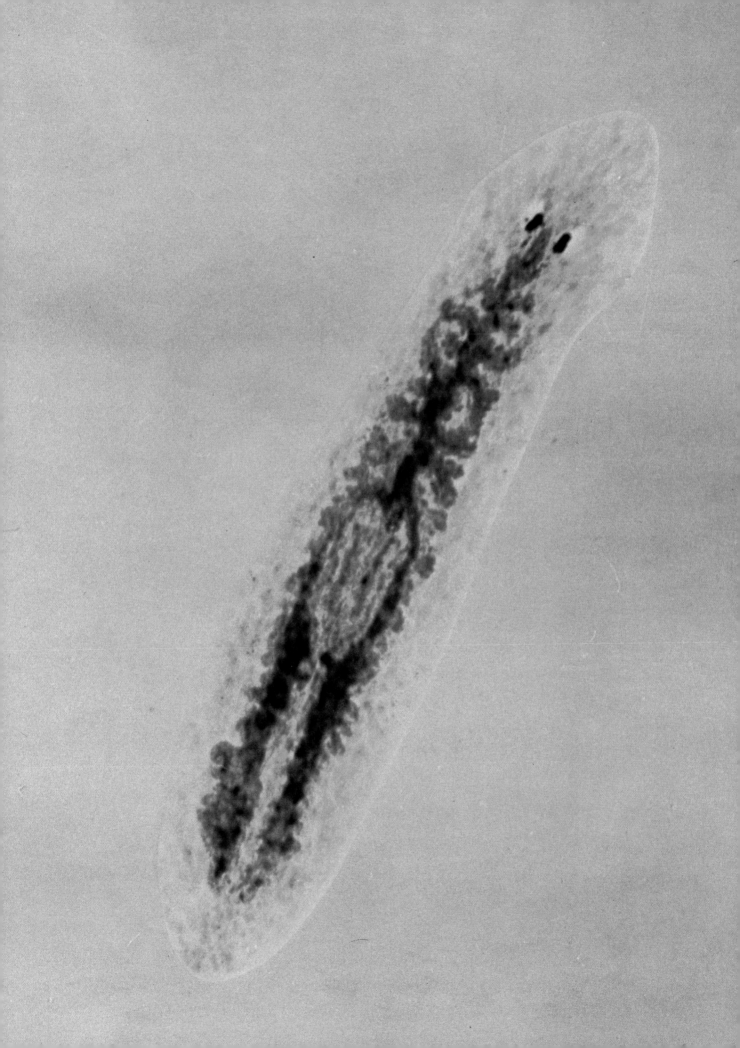

OCTOPUS ARM WITH SUCTION CUPS

This picture shows a cross section of one of the eight arms of an octopus. The section was taken through the center of a pair of suction cups. Each arm of the octopus has a double row of cups running down its length. The inner surface of each cup is made of a delicate tissue, which must be periodically replaced by a new growth. Transparent, paper-thin disks of skin are lost from the cups. An octopus in an aquarium may have dozens of these disks floating about him.

The suction cups are mainly used to grasp the animal's prey, which is primarily crabs. Each suction-lined arm has four layers of muscle, one layer on each side of the arm. Sometimes the octopus uses its arms for walking, but more often it moves through the water by jet propulsion. Water is taken in through the mouth and shot out of a tube behind the head, propelling the octopus forward in short bursts of speed. An octopus is slippery and almost impossible to catch by hand. If you try to hold one, it will shoot out of your hands like a bar of wet soap.

Octopuses are abundant on both the Atlantic and Pacific coasts, but they are not readily seen. The octopus is intelligent—it seems brighter than other invertebrate animals—and it usually keeps well hidden. Also, its color blends with its surroundings, and it can change colors rapidly to match those of rocks or sea plants, even speckled ones. A young, small octopus trapped by the retreating tide can usually be found quietly hiding in a pool under rocks or sea grass.

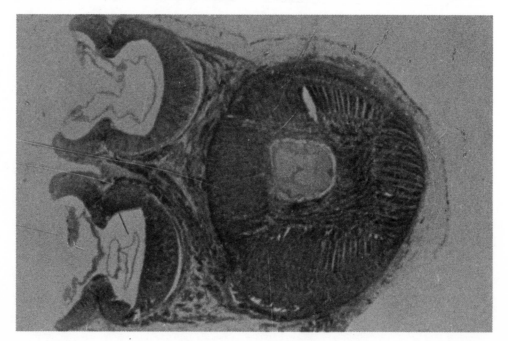

SHARK SCALES: OUTER SKELETON

Two kinds of fish swim in the seas of the world. Only the sharks and rays are cartilaginous *(kar-tih-LAJ-ih-nus)*; their skeletons are not bone, but cartilage like the bridge of a human nose. All others—trout, salmon, bass, tuna, and so on—are bony fish.

If you look closely at a shark, you will see that it does not have scales like a trout or salmon. The skin looks smooth. But if you have the opportunity of rubbing your hand over a shark's skin, it will feel rough, like sandpaper. This is because the skin is covered with tiny spines which project through the skin. These spines are attached to small plates, or plaques, just beneath the shark's skin. These placoid *(PLACK-oyd)* scales are not connected to each other, and only the spine is visible on the surface. The sharkskin in this picture has been specially treated to show the plates embedded in the skin.

Because placoid scales are made up of dentine and covered with enamel, it was once thought that they were the forerunners of teeth. Not only are they built like teeth, they line the mouths of sharks as well as the outer skin. But it is now known that placoid scales are actually the remains of the armorlike outer skeletons which once completely covered many kinds of ancient fish. These skeletons were made up of very large, heavy, scalelike plates. Sharks today are considered "living fossils," since they have remained unchanged for a very long time—almost fifty million years.

STARFISH PINCER

The small, pincerlike structures which the microscope reveals to us in this picture are called pedicellaria (*ped-ih-sell-LAY-ree-uh*). These tiny pincers are part of a starfish or sea star's protective coat. They grow all along the star's body, keeping it free of all debris.

Starfish have radial symmetry. Their arms, or rays, are arranged around a central disk. The skeleton of a starfish is on the outside of its body as the shark's used to be. It is covered with short, blunt spines that protect it from enemies. The spines are covered with skin, but often the skin is worn away and the white, spiny skeleton shows through. Between the spines are small, delicate gills with which the starfish breathes. The gills project through tiny openings, or pores, in the outer shell. The spines protect the gills to a certain degree, but it is the pedicellaria which keep the gills free of foreign matter that might damage them or interfere with breathing.

When a small animal creeps across the surface of the star, the pincers catch it in their jaws and pass it off the body before it can eat the exposed gills. The pincers also prevent plants from becoming attached to the starfish and sand from settling between its spines. Because of the pincers, starfish are always perfectly clean and free of "riders."

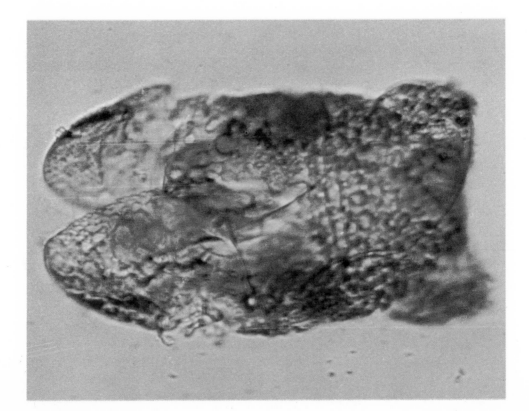

SEA BAT EGGS

Most animals that live in the ocean or along its shores lay their
eggs in the sea. The eggs seen here are those of a sea star found
along the Pacific coast. Its common name, the sea bat, comes from its
webbed rays. Its eggs are used in scientific research, especially in
embryology (em-bree-AHL-uh-jee), the study of the beginnings of a
creature's life. This is because adult sea bats' breeding season lasts
nearly all year, and as a result eggs are laid almost constantly.
Also, the large, brilliantly colored (red, yellow, or purple) bats are
easily found. They willingly produce large numbers of ripe eggs and
sperm in the laboratory. And the eggs are easily fertilized, developing
overnight into swimming star larvae.

Watching the beginning of a new life through the microscope, an
investigator at first sees only a single cell—the fertilized egg (the large
cell in the center of our picture). This one cell, fertilized by fresh
sperm, soon divides into two cells, then four, eight, and so on, until
there are hundreds of cells. This picture shows one-, two-, and
eight-celled stages formed by developing eggs. When the original egg
has divided into several hundreds of cells, we no longer speak of an
"egg" but of a developing individual, or embryo (EM-bree-oh). In a
short time that single cell will have produced skeleton and skin,
spines, gills, pincers, arms, and stomach. It will move, feed, breathe,
and produce eggs or sperm of its own. Though we can watch this
miracle of unfolding life, it still remains one of the great mysteries
of science.

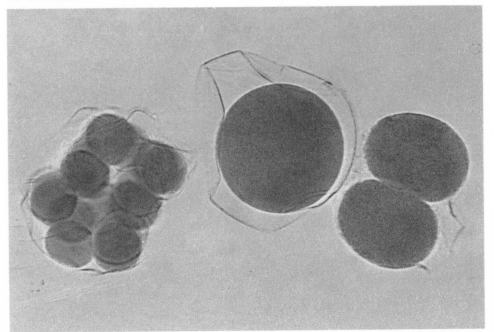

SALAMANDER DEVELOPMENT

No longer a uniform round ball of cells, this salamander egg has begun to form the final shape of the creature it will become. Cells are beginning to change according to the job they will preform in the full-grown individual. Nerve cells, muscle cells, digestive tissues, and so on develop a characteristic structure which can usually be seen at a very early stage.

Here is a series of longitudinal sections from a single salamander embryo. The salamander is an amphibian, a relative of the frog. You can see that it has a fishlike shape at this stage of development. The eyes are already well developed, and there is a definite mouth. In the tail section are the beginnings of the backbone.

Amphibians are the most primitive four-footed animals in existence. The frogs, toads, and salamanders living today are highly specialized remnants of the earliest amphibians, from which all land vertebrates (reptiles, birds, and mammals) have evolved. They have changed a great deal from their ancestors, but the life histories of individuals then and now are quite similar. The egg from which this salamander developed was small and, unlike those of birds and reptiles, had no protective membrane or shell. It was laid in water, like fish eggs. The embryo hatches from the egg as a tadpole, which undergoes a quick change when it reaches maturity. Its gills disappear and lungs and limbs develop as the salamander becomes a land animal. It must, however, forever live in moist places, since its lungs are inadequate for breathing and a good deal of oxygen must be absorbed through the salamander's moist skin.

SALAMANDER   DEVELOPMENT

Egg, 1 hour   80 hours   5½ days

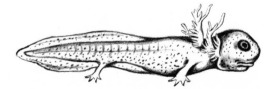

13 days

22 days, fully developed

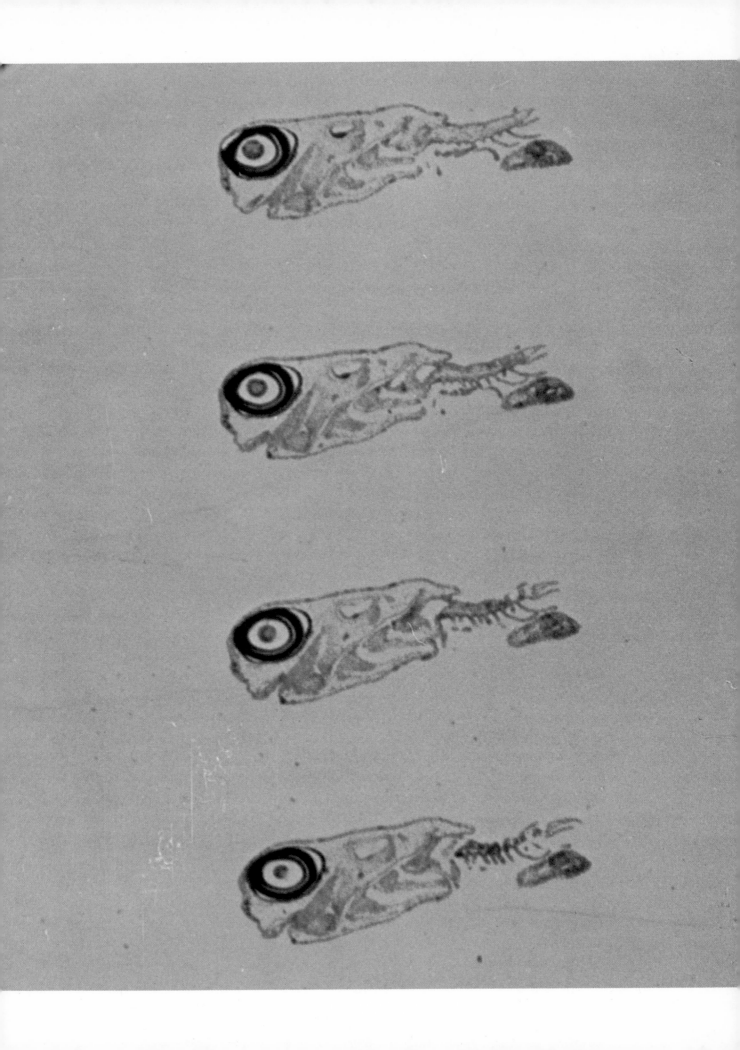

A CHICKEN EMBRYO

The chicken is a favorite subject of embryologists. Birds are closely related to man, and their embryonic development is quite like man's. Besides, chicken eggs are plentiful and relatively large.

Biologists have learned a great deal through such studies. This chicken embryo, forty-eight hours after fertilization, reveals the extraordinary beauty of unfolding life. It has taken millions of years of evolutionary development to produce this animal embryo. But with the microscope we can watch the results compressed into days.

The embryo is encased in the amnion (*AM-nee-on*), the innermost membrane enclosing the embryo, where the amniotic (*am-nee-OT-ik*) fluid protects it from drying and shock. Animals below the reptile level of evolutionary progress have eggs that develop and hatch in water; but the reptiles, birds, and mammals have their own private pools of amniotic fluid.

A chicken egg hatches twenty-one days after fertilization. This two-day embryo has only begun its development, and is still very tiny. But the chick is already taking shape. The developing brain is clearly visible at this stage. The eye is forming in the middle of the brain, and there is a fully formed lens already present within the eye. At this stage the heart appears as a transparent tube bent over on itself. The two main chambers of the heart are visible, and the heart is regularly pumping blood through the tiny chicken.

The embryo's food supply is the egg yolk in which the chick is suspended. There are thousands of tiny blood vessels spreading from the embryo through the yolk. These absorb food and oxygen, and carry them back to feed the rapidly growing chick.

An extension of the brain, the neural groove, runs down through the body. It will carry messages back and forth when it becomes the spinal cord. On either side of the neural groove are small blocks of cells, called somites, which will form the muscle structure. At this stage no legs or wings have developed, but in a matter of hours, tiny limb buds will begin to form.

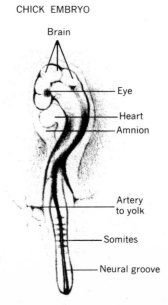

CHICK EMBRYO

Brain

Eye

Heart

Amnion

Artery to yolk

Somites

Neural groove

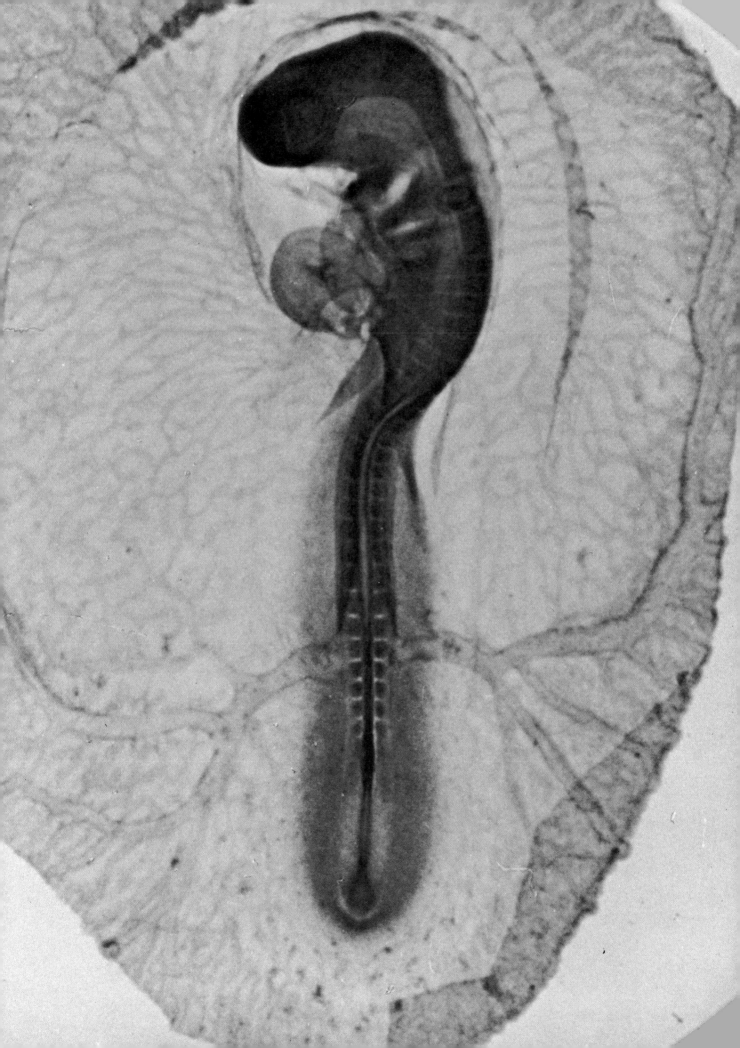

We know now that *all* animals show similarities during their early embryonic development. This is true even of those which are entirely different from one another as adults. The development of each individual repeats the history of its race. Today we see the evolution of hundreds of millions of years capsuled into days or weeks, as each animal climbs its own family tree. This "climbing" is so quick that the embryologist gets only a fleeting glimpse of even the most significant stages. For example, the gill slits in the human embryo, remnants of hundreds of millions of years of ocean ancestry, appear and then vanish in a matter of hours.

It is in such studies as embryology that man has uncovered, with the aid of the microscope, smaller and smaller units of life. And through such studies, man attempts to understand and control the living world around him — and to understand himself, too. The bacteriologist Theobald Smith once said: "We who have dealt with the infinitely small living things have perhaps as much a sense of the highly complex, the unfathomable, the eternally elusive in the universe, as do those who look for the outer boundaries of space. Each group contributes a different story to the same final significance."

BIBLIOGRAPHY

Here is a list of books which will tell you more about the limitless world to be viewed under the microscope.

Corrington, Julian D. *Exploring With Your Microscope.* New York: McGraw-Hill Book Co., Inc., 1957.

De Kruif, Paul. *Microbe Hunters.* New York: Pocket Books, Inc., 1959.

Grant, Madelein P. *Microbiology and Human Progress.* New York: Holt, Rinehart and Winston, Inc., 1953.

Harrison, C. William. *Microscope.* New York: Julian Messner, Inc., 1962.

Jacker, Corinne. *Window on the Unknown.* New York: Charles Scribner & Sons, 1967.

Krutch, Joseph Wood. *The Chain of Life.* Boston: Houghton Mifflin Co., 1956.

Mavor, James W. *General Biology.* New York: Macmillan Co., 1959.

Schneider, Leo. *Microbes in Your Life.* New York: Harcourt Brace & World, Inc., 1966.

——————. *You and Your Cells.* New York: Harcourt Brace & World, Inc., 1965.

Selsam, M. E. *Microbes at Work.* New York: William Morrow & Co., 1963.

Simon, J. *Microbes and Men.* New York: McGraw-Hill Book Co., 1966.

Storer, John H. *The Web of Life.* New York: Devin-Adair Co., 1953.

INDEX